To

Mum,

Thank you for being
who you are!

Love from

Debbie
x x x
x x
x

KT-447-460

Other books in this series:
Thank Heavens for Friends   For My Father
To my Grandmother with Love   Marriage a Keepsake
Love a Celebration   Words of Comfort

EDITED BY HELEN EXLEY
BORDERS BY SHARON BASSIN

*"For my mother Fay, who gave me the very greatest of gifts in
her precious love. For those days of Camelot.
With love forever from Sharon."*

"To my own dear mother, with all my love, Helen."

Published simultaneously in 1993 by Exley Publications in
Great Britain, and Exley Giftbooks in the USA.

12 11 10 9 8 7 6 5 4

Picture and text selection by © Helen Exley 1993.
Border Illustrations © Sharon Bassin 1993.
The moral right of the author has been asserted.

ISBN 1-85015-896-7

A copy of the CIP data is available from the British Library
on request.
Picture research by Image Select International.
Typeset by Delta, Watford.
Printed in China.

Exley Publications Ltd, 16 Chalk Hill, Watford,
Herts WD1 4BN, United Kingdom.

Exley Publications LLC, 232 Madison Avenue,
Suite 1206, NY 10016, USA.

For
MOTHER
a gift of love

A Helen Exley Giftbook

EXLEY
NEW YORK • WATFORD, UK

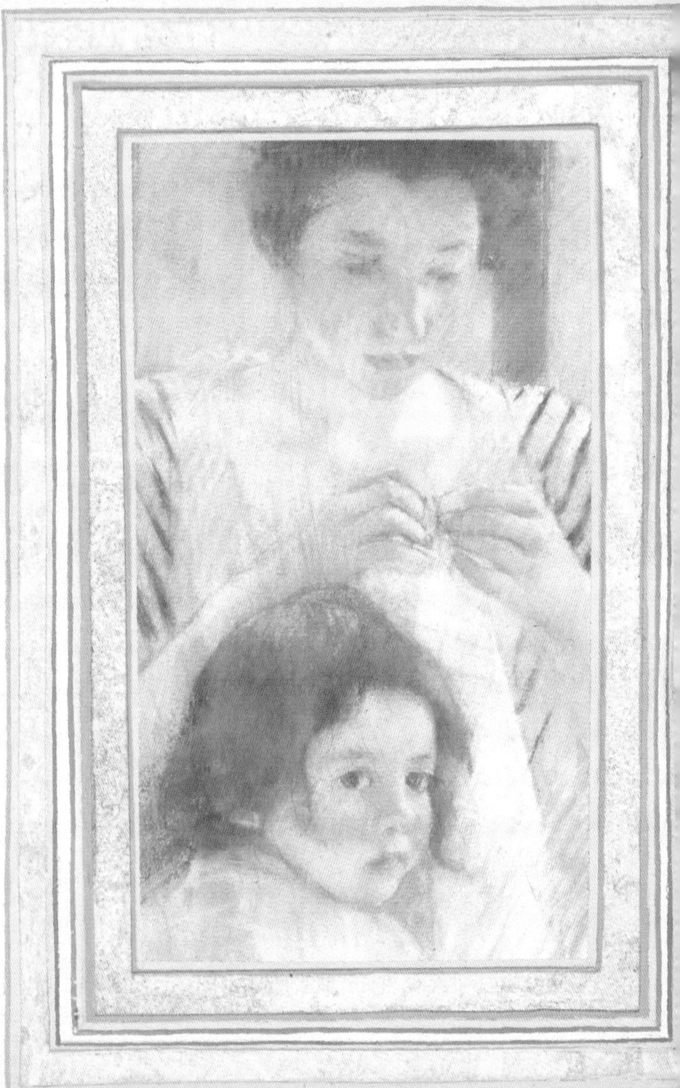

Mother, I love you so.
Said the child, I love you more than I know.
She laid her head on her mother's arm,
And the love between them kept them warm.

STEVIE SMITH

HAEC ORNAMENTA SUNT MEA

Cornelia, the mother of the Gracchi, once entertained a woman from Campania at her house. Since the woman made a great show of her jewels, which were among the most beautiful of the time, Cornelia detained her in conversation until her children came home from school. Then, pointing to her children, she said, "These are my jewels."

FROM "VALERIUS MAXIMUS" (1ST CENTURY)

Children, look into those eyes, listen to the dear
voice, notice the feeling of even a single touch
that is bestowed upon you by that gentle hand!
Make much of it while yet you have that most
precious of all good gifts, – a loving mother.
Read the unfathomable love of those eyes; the
kind anxiety of that tone and look, however slight
your pain. In after life you may have friends,
fond, dear friends, but never will you have again
the inexpressible love and gentleness lavished
upon you, which none but mother bestows.

THOMAS BABINGTON MACAULAY

I would desire for a friend the son who never resisted the tears of his mother.

LACRETALLE

A man loves his sweetheart the most, his wife the best, but his mother the longest.

IRISH PROVERB

Dear Mother. Never listens to an argument, never lets logic interfere with the warm impulses of her heart. Singing around the house, a girl's voice still, a bird's heart. Capricious, unpredictable, generous, tactless, stubborn, unreasonable, and lovable mother.

MAURICE WIGGIN

"The woman with happiness inside her" – this was the way of describing a pregnant woman.

OLD CHINESE

All that I am or hope to be, I owe to my angel mother.

ABRAHAM LINCOLN

My mother was the making of me. She was so true and so sure of me, I felt that I had someone to live for – someone I must not disappoint. The memory of my mother will always be a blessing to me.

THOMAS A. EDISON

Children do not know how their parents love them, and they never will till the grave closes over those parents, or till they have children of their own.

EDMUND VANCE COOKE

BECAUSE SHE IS A MOTHER

She broke the bread into fragments and gave them to the children, who ate with avidity.

"She hath kept none for herself," grumbled the Sergeant.

"Because she is not hungry," said a soldier.

"Because she is a mother," said the Sergeant.

VICTOR HUGO

THE HEROISM OF THE AVERAGE MOTHER

How many thousands of heroines there must be now, of whom we shall never know. But still they are there. They sow in secret the seed of which we pluck the flower, and eat the fruit, and know not that we pass the sower daily in the streets.

One form of heroism – the most common, and yet the least remembered of all – namely, the heroism of the average mother. Ah! When I think of that broad fact, I gather hope again for poor humanity; and this dark world looks bright – this diseased world looks wholesome to me once more – because, whatever else it is not full of, it is at least full of mothers.

Charles Kingsley

MOTHER COURAGE

In the wake of every evil inflicted by man or nature come the women, gathering what can be salvaged, the distraught and injured children, the lost, the dispossessed, the fragments of a broken society. They stoop across every battlefield, seeking for their own. They tear at blocks of stone tumbled by earthquake, blackened by fire. They build among the olive trees or the desert sand.

Out of destruction they piece together small areas of safety, letting fragments stand as symbols of a whole. Here is a house, patched out of cardboard; here is a kitchen, stocked with rusted cans. Here is a cradle in a nest of rags. The earth erupts, the typhoon sweeps away a clutch of villages, the causes rage across the landscape, the bitter wire divides. But the women crouch beside their fires and hide the children in their shawls. They have suffered too much in making life to let it go so easily; they cannot think in cold statistics or see the death of any child as a necessity.

PAMELA BROWN

A GIFT FOR MAMA

... I have been worrying for weeks now about what to give my mother for Mother's Day. For most people this is a modest problem, solved by the purchase of a box of chocolates. For me, however, Mother's Day represents an annual challenge to do the impossible – find a gift that will make neither Mama nor me feel terrible.

Expensive gifts are out, because they make Mama feel terrible. "This is awful," she says, examining an apron. "I feel just terrible. You shouldn't have spent the money on me." Inexpensive presents please Mama, but they make *me* feel terrible.

There is always the danger a gift given to Mama will bounce swiftly back to the giver. If I buy her something to wear, she perceives in an instant that it could be let in here, let out there, and it would fit me perfectly. If I give her a plant, she cuts off the top for me to take home and root in a glass of water.

If I give her something edible, she wants me to stay for lunch and eat it.

Papa, a sensible man, long ago stopped trying to shop for Mama. Instead, on Mother's Day, her birthday and other appropriate occasions, he composes for her a short epic poem in which he tells of their meeting, courtship and subsequent marriage. After nearly thirty years of poems, Papa sometimes worries that the edge of his poetic inspiration has dulled, but Mama doesn't complain. She comes into the room while he is struggling over a gift poem and says, "It doesn't have to rhyme, as long as it's from the heart."

This year, finally, I think I too have found a painless gift for Mama. I am going to give her a magazine article, unrhymed but from the heart, in which I wish her "Happy Mother's Day", and tell her that there's nothing Papa or I could ever buy, find or make for her that would be half good enough, anyway.

HELENE MELYAN, FROM AN ARTICLE IN "THE OREGONIAN"

Few of us, if any, are so fortunate as to be able to look back to any time in our lives with regret, because we were too dutiful, gentle, kind, and generous to our good mothers. On the contrary, most of us if not all, have heartaches, when too late, we wish we were more loving, more dutiful, more thoughtful in every way, to give pleasure, when we could; so that this day is intended to bring to our mind a more active thought, to make the lives of our mothers happier and brighter, and to see where we can improve on the past.

Very often our good mothers hunger and yearn for the loving thoughts which every true mother cherishes. Often a good mother's life is filled with emptiness: because of love never shown, and letters from the absent son and daughter that never come. And yet no man or woman is too poor or too busy to remember this devoted parent.

Mother's Day is to remind us of our duty before it is too late.

L. L. LOAN, ON THE FIRST MOTHER'S DAY

I remember the flash of insight I had in 1940 as I sat talking to a small delegation that had come to ask me to address a women's congress. I had my baby on my lap, and as we talked I recalled my psychology professor's explanation of why women are less productive than men. He had referred to a letter written by Harriet Beecher Stowe in which she said that she had in mind to write a novel about slavery, but the baby cried so much. It suddenly occurred to me that it would have been much more plausible if she had said "but the baby smiles so much." It is not that women have less impulse than men to be creative and productive. But through the ages having children, for women who wanted children, has been so satisfying that it has taken some special circumstance – spinsterhood, barrenness, or widowhood – to let women give their whole minds to other work.

Margaret Mead

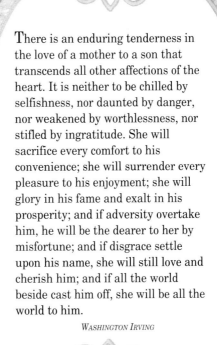

There is an enduring tenderness in the love of a mother to a son that transcends all other affections of the heart. It is neither to be chilled by selfishness, nor daunted by danger, nor weakened by worthlessness, nor stifled by ingratitude. She will sacrifice every comfort to his convenience; she will surrender every pleasure to his enjoyment; she will glory in his fame and exalt in his prosperity; and if adversity overtake him, he will be the dearer to her by misfortune; and if disgrace settle upon his name, she will still love and cherish him; and if all the world beside cast him off, she will be all the world to him.

WASHINGTON IRVING

SHE WORKS AT TASKS

She works at tasks
Requiring no especial skill,
Yet making their demands,
Hard to fulfil,
Demands on time and patience
And the capricious will.

Grease blears the gaze
Of water cooling in the bowl
And films her wrists and hands;
Toil takes its toll
Of strength, drains light and music
From the air and numbs the soul;

Or surely would
Except her love re-makes all
  things,
And every trivial chore,
Transmuted, brings
A sacramental joy
And, while she works, she sings.

VERNON SCANNELL

No matter how old a mother is she watches her middle-aged children for signs of improvement.

FLORIDA SCOTT-MAXWELL

At eighty-eight the mother of the Parrish children was still working in Hollywood as an extra. "She won't take a taxi, too expensive and we took her car away from her a few years ago," said Parrish. "So my brother, who is a senior vice-president for Coca-Cola, will be in conference and the phone will ring.

'Gordon, will you drive me over to Universal?' And he drops everything and does it."

You see, it's never easy to say no to a genuine stage mother.

FROM "GROWING UP IN HOLLYWOOD" BY ROBERT PARRISH

A CLASSIC

When the son leaves home to start his freshman year at college, his doting mother gives him two cashmere sweaters as going-away presents. Wanting to show his appreciation the boy comes home for Thanksgiving wearing one of the sweaters.

The mother greets him at the door. She takes a long, anxious look and says: "What's the matter? The other sweater you didn't like?"

LIZ SMITH

It was reported that a 123-pound woman, Mrs. Maxwell Rogers, lifted one end of a 3,600lb. (1.60 tons) stationwagon which, after the collapse of a jack, had fallen on top of her son at Tampa, Florida, on 24 April 1960. She cracked some vertebrae.

FROM "THE GUINNESS BOOK OF RECORDS"

In the eyes of its mother every beetle is a gazelle.

MOROCCAN PROVERB

When you havva no babies, you havva nothing.

ITALIAN IMMIGRANT WOMAN

the worst to be said
   about mothers
   is that they
   are prone
      to give
      kisses
   of con-
   grat-
   u-
   lation
which make you feel
   like a battleship
   on which someone
   is breaking
      a bottle.

NORMAN MAILER

What was locked in that extremity of expression that I so loved as a child? When the grown-ups became annoyed with our childish fights and shrieks and sent us out of the house yelling, "Go play in the traffic!" Why did I feel deeply secure, certain of their undying love? Was it that by their yelling, their faces puffing red, their fingers pointing dramatically toward the door, their hateful words screaming at the tops of their lungs, that I knew how much they loved us? Yes, it was that. But it was more. I sensed, I now know, that they, by their own expression, acknowledged the devil in us all, established their toleration for the reality of our humanness. "You are my hell on earth, my endless burden!" the mother shrieks at the child she patently adores. And the child, if not the neighbors, hears the silent addition: "my reason for staying alive."

JANE LAZARRE IN "VILLAGE VOICE"

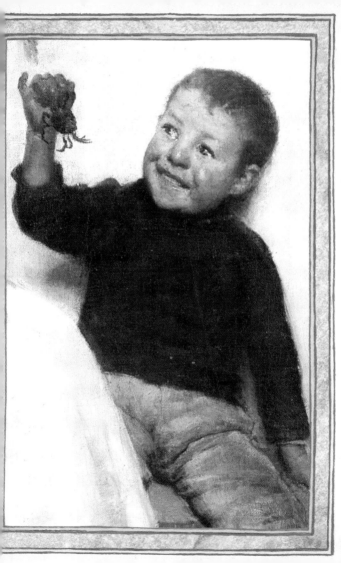

FROM A LETTER TO HER DAUGHTER

I can remember the exact moment you were conceived and shouted aloud and exulted with perhaps the most perfect feeling I've ever had. It was under the trees in the middle of the day during the war when I was camp following. Your dad had a couple of hours off and we had gone for a drive. And I said – that's my new baby. And it's always going to love the sky through the trees and the birds and the smell of grass and earth and busy insects and rising trunks and togetherness. And so it has happened.

Of course I thought I could never love my second baby as much as I had loved my first, but from the moment I held you in my arms I had a surge of mother love that outweighed any feelings of doubt.

It has been the same with my grandchildren. I adored Lincoln with all my heart. Then I thought, I will try, but I can't love Dalton just as much. Well, of course, he went into my heart with such violence that he is there on top, boots and all. (No, flat feet at all.)

When Sue was on the way, I decided to try my

best not to discriminate – but, what do you know, from the first moment my heart expanded to take her in. Each passing year she gives more to me and I love her more – which of course is impossible – because I loved her with all my heart all the time.

Then came Jeff – now I was sure he was an also-ran. Well, he is such a charmer and so gentle and, well just Jeff, that I can't help it – he occupies all my heart, just like the others.

Oh, dear – then came Gareth, the last. Well, he just looked so adorable and well, I just loved him. He was a difficult baby and for a few months I felt sorry for him because he cried a lot, and so I loved him more to make up for what seemed wrong. Now he is the most humorous strong active loving child you could imagine.

I know you don't like to say "all my love", but I do. I use it with discrimination, but it certainly embraces both my children, both my children-in-law and my five grandchildren. I have other loves, for relations and friends, but this all-pervasive love that draws us together is limited to these few, and still embraces my own Pop and Mom.

MARION GARRETTY

WALKING AWAY

It is eighteen years ago, almost to the day –
A sunny day with the leaves just turning,
The touch-lines new-ruled – since I watched you
    play
Your first game of football, then, like a satellite
Wrenched from its orbit, go drifting away

Behind a scatter of boys, I can see
You walking away from me towards the school
With the pathos of a half-fledged thing set free
Into a wilderness, the gait of one
Who finds no path where the path should be.

That hesitant figure, eddying away
Like a winged seed loosened from its parent
    stem,
Has something I never quite grasp to convey
About nature's give-and-take – the small, the
    scorching
Ordeals which fire one's irresolute clay.

I have had worse partings, but none that so
    Gnaws at my mind still. Perhaps it is roughly
Saying what God alone could perfectly show –
How selfhood begins with a walking away,
And love is proved in the letting go.

C. DAY LEWIS

THE MOTHER

There will be a singing in your heart,
There will be a rapture in your eyes;
You will be a woman set apart,
You will be so wonderful and wise.
You will sleep, and when from dreams you start
As of one that wakes in Paradise
There will be a singing in your heart,
There will be a rapture in your eyes.

There will be a moaning in your heart,
There will be an anguish in your eyes,
You will see your dearest ones depart,
You will hear their quivering good-byes.

Yours will be the heart-ache and the smart,
Tears that scald and lonely sacrifice;
There will be a moaning in your heart,
There will be an anguish in your eyes.

There will come a glory in your eyes,
There will come a peace within your heart;
Sitting 'neath the quiet evening skies,
Time will dry the tear and dull the smart.
You will know that you have played your part;
Yours shall be the love that never dies:
You, with Heaven's peace within your heart,
You, with God's own glory in your eyes.

ROBERT SERVICE

All mothers are rich when they love their
  children.
There are no poor mothers, no ugly ones, no old
  ones.
Their love is always the most beautiful of the
  joys.
And when they seem most sad, it needs but a
  kiss which they receive or give to turn all
  their tears into stars . . .

MAURICE MAETERLINCK

THE CHAIR IN WHICH YOU'VE SAT

The chair in which you've sat's not just a chair
nor the table at which you've eaten just a table
nor the window that you've looked from just a
   window.
All these have now a patina of your
body and mind, a kind of ghostly glow which
haloes them a little, though invisible.

IAIN CRICHTON SMITH

As years ago we carried to your knees
The tales and treasures of eventful days,
Knowing no deed too humble for your praise,
Nor any gift too trivial to please,
So still we bring, with older smiles and tears,
What gifts we may, to claim the old, dear right;
Your faith, beyond the silence and the night,
Your love still close and watching through the
    years.

KATHLEEN NORRIS

Sonnets are full of love, and this my tome
    Has many sonnets: so here now shall be
    One sonnet more, a loving sonnet from me
To her whose heart is my heart's quiet home,
    To my first Love, my Mother on whose knee
I learnt love-lore that is not troublesome:
    Whose service is my special dignity
And she my lodestar while I go and come.
And so because you love, and because
    I love you, Mother, I have woven a wreath
Of rhymes wherewith to crown your honoured
        name:
    In you not fourscore years can dim the flame
Of love, whose blessed glow transcends the laws
    Of time and change and mortal life and death.

CHRISTINA G. ROSSETTI

A LONG PARTING

You have been long from me
and I have tried to treat your
   absence as normality,
and live as once I did before
   you came;
but now your hands hold mine
and all the years are gone
and all the hidden pain,
and I'm complete again.

CHARLOTTE GRAY

MOTHER O'MINE

If I were hanged on the highest hill,
   Mother o'mine, O mother o'mine!
I know whose love would follow me still,
   Mother o'mine, O mother o'mine!
If I were drowned in the deepest sea,
   Mother o'mine, O mother o'mine!

I know whose tears would come down to me,
   Mother o'mine, O mother o'mine!
If I were damned by body and soul,
I know whose prayers would make me whole,
   Mother o'mine, O mother o'mine!

RUDYARD KIPLING

Hey kids! Remember me?
I'm the lady with the Christmas tree.
I'm the lady with the beard and sack . . .

Waved you off and hugged you back.
Packed your bags and waited up . . .

Bought you a bicycle. Bought you a pup.

Kissed you better and blew your noses
Bottled you jam and picked you roses.

Legs gone shaky; stuck in a chair.
Not too sure about when or where.
Don't quite know how I got like this . . .

Send me a letter . . .

Send me a kiss.

PAMELA BROWN

You will have the road gate open, the front
   door ajar
The kettle boiling and a table set
By the window looking out at the sycamores –
And your loving heart lying in wait

For me coming up among the poplar trees.
You'll know my breathing and my walk
And it will be a summer evening on those roads
Lonely with leaves of thought.

We will be choked with the grief of things
   growing,
The silence of dark-green air
Life too rich – the nettles, docks and thistles
All answering the prodigal's prayer.

You will know I am coming though I send no
   word
For you were lover who could tell
A man's thoughts – my thoughts – though I hid
   them –
Through you I knew Woman and did not fear
   her spell.

PATRICK KAVANAGH

. . . Fifty-four years of love and tenderness and crossness and devotion and unswerving loyalty. Without her I could only have achieved a quarter of what I have achieved, not only in terms of success and career, but in terms of personal happiness. We have quarrelled, often violently, over the years, but she has never stood between me and my life, never tried to hold me too tightly, always let me go free. For a woman of her strength of character this was truly remarkable. There was no fear in her except for me. She was a great woman to whom I owe the whole of my life.

NOËL COWARD

. . . Children, children,
Why do we ever have children?
They only grow up and they leave one day
And they blame us for taking their dreams
    away,
And the houses are empty, the nurseries
    forlorn,
These were beautiful places when they were born.
Children, children,
What can you say about children?
Who knows where their childhood ends,
Or when it ends,
Just why you drift apart.
I only know that they never leave your heart.

HAL SHAPER

Acknowledgements: The publishers gratefully acknowledge permission to reproduce copyright material, and would be interested to hear from any copyright holders not here acknowledged.

NOEL COWARD, extract from *Remembered Laughter,* published by Jonathan Cape on behalf of the Noel Estate; IAIN CRICHTON SMITH, "The Chair in which You've Sat". Reprinted from *Love Poems & Elegies* by permission of Victor Gollancz Ltd; C. DAY LEWIS "Walking Away" from *The Gate* published by Jonathan Cape. Reprinted by permission of Sinclair Stevenson Reed; Extract from *The Guinness Book of Records,* copyright © Guinness Publishing Ltd., Guinness is a registered trademark of Guinness Publishing Ltd.; PATRICK KAVANAGH, "In Memory of My Mother". Reprinted from *The Collected Poems of Patrick Kavanagh* by permission of the publishers, Martin Brian & O'Keefe Ltd, and Mrs Katherine Kavanagh; JANE LAZARRE, extract from *Village Voice.* Reprinted by permission of the author's agent, Wendy Weil; NORMAN MAILER, "The worst to be said..." from *Deaths for the Ladies (and other Disasters).* Reprinted by permission of the author's agent, Scott Meredith Literary Agency, Inc., MARGARET MEAD, extract from *Blackberry Winter: My earlier years,* Reprinted by permission of Angus & Robertson UK Ltd, an imprint of Harper Collins Publishers Ltd, and William Morrow & Co. Inc.; HELENE MELYAN, "A Gift for Mama". Reprinted with permission from the March 1978 "Reader's Digest" and "The Oregonian", Portland, Oregon; KATHLEEN NORRIS, "As years ago we carried to your knees"; ROBERT PARRISH, extract *Growing up in Hollywood.* Reprinted by permission of Robert Parrish; VERNON SCANNELL, "She works at tasks" from *The Loving Game* published by Robson Books Ltd. Reprinted by permission of the publishers; ROBERT SERVICE, "The Mother" from *Rhymes of a Rolling Stone.* Reprinted by permission of Feinman and Krasilovsky p.c.; HAL SHAPER, from "Children" from the musical version of *Great Expectations.* Reprinted by permission of Hal Shaper and the Sparta Florida Music Group Ltd; LIZ SMITH, extract from *The Mother Book.* Reprinted by permission of Granada Publishing, an imprint of HarperCollins Publishers Ltd and Gloria Safer; Stevie Smith, "Human Affection" from *The Collected Poems* published by Allen Lane. Reprinted by permission of James MacGibbon, executor of the Stevie Smith Estate; MAURICE WIGGIN, "Dear Mother never listens to an argument" from *Compliments* by G. Polickman. Reprinted by permission of George Allen & Unwin, now Unwin Hyman, an imprint of HarperCollins Publishers Ltd. Picture Credits: Alinari: cover. Archiv Fur Kunst: title page Dora Hitz – "Das Sonnen Kind" and pages 19, 29, 31, 39, 44/45, 51, 53, 55, 59 © DACS Cuno Amiet: Die blaue Landschaft. Chris Beetles Gallery: page 49. Bridgeman Art Library: pages 10, 12, 17, 24, 35, 44/45, 61. Fine Art Photographic Library: pages 23, 27, 32/33, 43, 56. Giraudon: pages 6 © Mary Cassat "Mother & Child". Haworth Art Gallery, Lancs: page 16. Louvre Museum, Paris: page 31. Nasjonalgalleriet, Oslo: page 46. National Gallery of Art, Washington DC: page 31. Scala: pages 9, 15, 40/41. Skagens Museum, Denmark: pages 10, 11. Towneley Hall Art Gallery and Museum, Burnley: page 24, 61. Whitford and Hughes, London: page 35.